CHINA

Marshall Cavendish
Benchmark
New York

This edition first published in 2011 in
the United States of America by
Marshall Cavendish Benchmark.

Marshall Cavendish Benchmark
99 White Plains Road
Tarrytown, NY 10591
Website: www.marshallcavendish.us

© Marshall Cavendish International (Asia)
Pte Ltd 2011
Originated and designed by Marshall Cavendish
International (Asia) Pte Ltd
A member of Times Publishing Limited
Times Centre, 1 New Industrial Road
Singapore 536196

Written by: Colin Cheong
Edited by: Crystal Chan
Designed by: Lock Hong Liang
Picture research: Thomas Khoo

Library of Congress Cataloging-in-Publication Data
Cheong, Colin.
China / By Colin Cheong.
p. cm. -- (Festivals of the world)
Includes bibliographical references and index.
Summary: "This book explores the exciting culture
and many festivals that are celebrated in China"--
Provided by publisher.
ISBN 978-1-60870-096-7
1. Festivals--China--Juvenile literature. 2. China--
Social life and customs--Juvenile literature. I. Title.
GT4883.A2C484 2011
394.26951--dc22
2010000212
ISBN 978-1-60870-096-7

Printed in Malaysia

1 3 6 5 4 2

Contents

It's Festival Time . . .

The word *festival* in Chinese is 节日 [JYEH-reh]. The Chinese have been celebrating festivals for thousands of years. Each one is rich in tradition and is important to Chinese culture. In China there are colorful and exciting festivals about dragons, the lady in the moon, and even how to take care of ghosts. So get ready for an adventure. It's 节日 time in China!

Where's China?

China lies in the middle of Asia, between India in the west and Korea and Japan in the east. There are rolling hills, wide plains, and high plateaus in China. The soil is rich in the eastern part of the country, and farming is an important activity there. Most of the people live in the east. The southwest is covered with tall mountains. In the northwest, there are many deserts. Few people live in these remote areas. There are many different climates in China. In the south, it can be as warm as Hawaii, while some northern regions can be as cold as Alaska.

Who Are the Chinese?

About one in every five people in the world lives in China. The earliest Chinese people lived around the Huang He, or Yellow River, where the land is good for farming. For centuries, China was divided into warring states before being united under one emperor. There were also periods when China was conquered by foreign invaders. Most of the people in China are **Han Chinese**, but there are also over fifty other groups. The Zhuang, Bai,

✳ A young boy from Shanghai, the second largest city in China (Beijing is the biggest). There are more people in China than in any other country in the world.

Dai, Tibetans, and Mongolians are just a few. These people mostly live in the desert and mountain areas. Many Chinese have moved to other countries, such as Taiwan, Singapore, and the United States. They are called overseas Chinese. Most Chinese follow a religion that is a combination of **Buddhism** and **Taoism**, but some of the smaller groups are **Muslim** or Christian.

＊ The Great Wall of China was built many centuries ago to keep out China's enemies. It runs for thousands of miles across northern China.

What Are the Festivals?

China uses two types of calendars—the Gregorian calendar and a **lunar** calendar. The Gregorian calendar is used for things like work and school, while the lunar calendar is used for most festivals. Chinese festivals do not always fall on the same date or even the same month on the Gregorian calendar.

> It's party time! Come to the Lantern Festival.

> Meet you on the moon!

SPRING

* **Chinese New Year**—China's biggest festive celebration of the entire lunar calendar.

* **Dai Water Splashing Festival**—Dai people splash water on each other to give blessings and wish happiness.

* **Lantern Festival**—Hundreds of lanterns are lit to celebrate the first full moon of the year.

* **Qingming** (Pure Brightness Festival)—People clean their **ancestors'** graves and set out offerings as a mark of respect.

* **Birthday of Tian Hou, Goddess of the Sea**—Particularly popular among sailors, this festival is a big event in San Francisco, Hong Kong, and Taiwan. There are lion dancers, stilt walkers, and acrobats.

SUMMER

* **Dragon Boat Festival**—A day marked by exciting dragon boat races and feasts that include rice dumpling

Come celebrate New Year's Day with us in Tibet.

AUTUMN

✳ **The Cowherd and the Weaving Maid Festival**—A festival with sewing competitions.

✳ **Hungry Ghosts Festival**—People make offerings to visiting ghosts for a month before they return to the other world.

✳ **Mid-Autumn Festival**—The moon is believed to be at its fullest and brightest in the middle of autumn. The occasion is marked with outdoor picnics and feasting on moon cakes.

✳ **Double-Ninth Festival**—A day to have picnics and drink chrysanthemum wine to celebrate the coming of winter.

✳ **National Day**—Huge parades and celebrations in Beijing to celebrate the birthday of the People's Republic of China.

WINTER

✳ **Winter Solstice Festival**—The Thanksgiving Day of the Chinese calendar and the time when *tang yuan* are cooked.

Join in the dragon dance!

Chinese New Year

Firecrackers, loud drumming, and clashing cymbals welcome the biggest festival of the Chinese calendar. This is the Spring Festival, or Chinese New Year, as it is commonly known. The huge celebration usually lasts several days.

Cleaning and Cooking

People prepare for the new year by cleaning their houses. They do this to get rid of all the bad luck collected in the past year. During the first days of the new year, people stop cleaning so that they won't sweep all the new luck away! Also, before the festival, Chinese families prepare enough food to last at least three days. Using a knife during the first days of the new year is considered bad luck. More importantly, people must pay off all their debts and settle all their quarrels with people they know so they can begin the new year with a fresh start.

* This girl is dressed up in her New Year's best. For the New Year, everyone dresses in bright colors, especially red because it is considered auspicious, or lucky.

The Kitchen God Is Sent Off

A week before the New Year holiday, many people prepare a big feast for the Kitchen God—a well-known character in Chinese folklore.

According to the folktale, there was once a man who left his wife for a younger woman. His new wife spent all his money and left him to beg for food. When he was begging, he came to the house of a kind woman, who gave him food. When he saw that the woman was his first wife, he was so ashamed he jumped into an oven. Because the man recognized his wrongdoing, he was made into the Kitchen God.

All year long, it is believed that the Kitchen God watches over the fortunes of the family. Then, on the twenty-third day of the last month of the year, he is given a feast and sent off to tell the Jade Emperor, the highest god in Taoism, about the family. On this day, families usually smear the mouth of a statue of the Kitchen God with honey so that he will have only sweet things to say about the family.

For the New Year, older family members give children red envelopes with money inside, called *hongbao*. By the end of the holiday, some children have received a lot of money from parents, grandparents, aunts, uncles, and others.

Keeping Monsters Away

Everything is decorated in red for the New Year. There's an old Chinese story that explains why. A long time ago, according to the tale, there was a terrible monster called the *nian* that came to a village at the end of every winter and gobbled up all of the villagers. Then a wise man told the people that the monster was afraid of three things: noise, bright lights, and the color red. So the people lit a bonfire, set off fireworks, and painted their doors red. From then on, the nian no longer bothered them. Today people continue to decorate their houses with red banners to protect against evil spirits. In addition, setting off firecrackers is one of the favorite pastimes of the New Year celebration.

✳ People put up lots of decorations for the New Year. The most popular are long strips of red paper with wishes of good luck painted on them. These are hung next to the doors of their homes.

✳ Children with painted faces are ready to take part in a New Year's parade. Many people go to see a fortune-teller on New Year's Day to find out what the new year will bring.

Rich Foods and Healthy Words

Chinese New Year is a time when everyone is careful to say and do only good things to bring luck to the family in the next year. At the big meal on New Year's Eve, each dish has a name that brings to mind health or riches, like Broth of Prosperity or Silvery Threads of Longevity. People also eat sweetened **kumquats** because part of the Chinese name for kumquats means gold. Another traditional food is dumplings. Some of the dumplings have copper coins cooked in them to bring luck. Everyone goes around wishing everyone else "gong xi fa cai," which means wishing you prosperity.

✳ On New Year's Eve, families get together for a big feast. That night, children are allowed to stay up late. It is thought that the longer they stay up, the longer their parents will live.

THINK ABOUT THIS

Do you do anything special on New Year's Day to bring luck in the coming year? Many cultures have traditions to bring good luck. For instance, many Americans believe they should eat black-eyed peas on New Year's Day.

The Lantern Festival

Fifteen days after the beginning of the Chinese New Year comes the first full moon of the year. This is the Feast of the First Full Moon, also known as the Lantern Festival. The Lantern Festival began as a celebration of the light and warmth of the Sun after winter. Today it takes place on the last night of the New Year's festival. People leave their homes to look at the hundreds of lanterns hanging in the streets. The lanterns come in all sorts of shapes—boxes, globes, animals, and many other forms. Acrobats, jugglers, stilt walkers, and others perform in the streets to mark the occasion.

✳ In Fujian Province, some families light as many lanterns as there are people in the family. If they want more children, they light extra lanterns.

Remember to Feed the Lions

Lion dancers are a favorite part of the New Year's and Lantern festivals. Two young men from a **martial arts** school stand inside a lion costume. They move around inside to make the lion jump, lie down, and roll over. To make it rear up on its hind legs, the man in the front jumps on the other man's shoulders. Musicians beat on large drums and gongs as the lion bounces around. People invite lion dancers to their homes or shops to bring good luck in the coming year. They put out oranges and **hongbao** for the lion dancers. The lion pretends to eat the oranges and hongbao and then spits out the peels. The money from the hongbao is then used to support the martial arts school.

✳ Acrobats and others perform in Beijing. In dry boat plays, performers dress up in costumes that hide their legs and look like boats. They pretend to be children picking lotus flowers on a lake.

Watch out for the lion!

These masked figures are a part of a celebration for the Lantern Festival.

Dancing Dragons

The highlight of the festivities is the dragon dance. The dragon is made out of paper or silk stretched over a bamboo frame. It is held up on poles by a dozen or more people who run together, making the dragon wind through the streets. One person holds a yellow or red globe for the dragon to chase. This is a symbol for the Sun. It is thought that if the dragon catches it, the Sun will go out. The dragon dance ends in a burst of sparkling fireworks. In the past, people believed the dragon controlled the clouds, rain, and rivers. The dragon dance celebrates the spring rain and the Sun.

✳ The Chinese dragon has the body of a snake, the head, mane, and tail of a horse, the paws of a dog, the horns of a deer, the scales and whiskers of fish, and the wings of a bird. Long ago, before China was one country, different tribes worshiped different animals. When the tribes were united, they joined parts of their animals into a single creature—the dragon.

Bai girls perform a dance for the Lantern Festival in Yunnan Province. Many of the other groups of peoples in China celebrate the same festivals as the Han Chinese.

Dragons Abroad

For many years, traditional festivals were quietly celebrated in China. People stayed at home and had special meals with their families. In recent years, China's government has helped bring back traditional festivals as a way to celebrate Chinese culture.

In other countries, Chinese people have worked hard to keep traditions alive. Each year, the biggest dragon parade in the world is held in San Francisco, California.

THINK ABOUT THIS

You can find dragons in the myths of almost every culture in the world. In Europe, Christian saints were portrayed fighting dragons. In Africa and India, dragons were believed to help sustain the world. In Mexico, the "plumed serpent," which looks a lot like a dragon, was an important god.

Ghost Festivals

In Chinese culture, older relatives must be treated with respect—even after they have died. Many Chinese believe that after a person dies, his or her spirit lives on and is aware of what is happening in the world of the living. Spirits are believed to be powerful, so people try to make them happy. They do this by remembering them, offering them food, and burning **incense**. If an ancestor's spirit is pleased, he or she might bring good luck.

Qingming

A big part of the Qingming Festival is remembering ancestors and making sure they are happy in the afterlife. People offer food to the dead. They also burn paper money and other offerings. A common belief is that burning something sends it to the spirit world, where the dead can use it.

✳ This person is leaving food for an ancestor. Qingming is one of the few holidays that is on the Gregorian calendar. It falls on April 4.

Festival Beginnings

Qingming means pure brightness in Chinese. The festival was originally a celebration of springtime. People would leave their villages and travel to the countryside to walk on the new grass. Then people stopped to clean graves in the hills around the village.

A Good Time to Fly a Kite

Qingming is a time to rejoice in life. One activity is especially popular—kite flying. Kites have a special place in Chinese history. Long ago, according to legend, the states of Chu and Han were at war. Xin, the Han general, made a kite big enough for a warrior to ride in. The warrior used the kite to fly over the Chu camp singing Chu songs. Hearing songs from home made the Chu warriors so sad that they surrendered and went home.

✳ Bai people in Yunnan Province making offerings to their ancestors.

✳ The dragon kite is a Chinese invention. It is difficult to fly but quite spectacular to see.

Visits from Hungry Ghosts

Some Chinese believe that on the first day of the seventh lunar month, the spirits are allowed to wander the world for a month. There are many spirits that are believed to have no one to offer them food and presents. These spirits may become angry and cause mischief, so people leave offerings for the stray ghosts. They leave food and incense by the roadside. They also burn paper "spirit" money so the ghosts will have some spending money in the other world. This is called the Hungry Ghosts Festival.

Sticks of incense, called joss sticks, are burned to take prayers up to the spirit world. At funerals, the Chinese often burn paper models of things the dead person might need, such as a car, a house, or money.

＊ Chinese opera is very popular, especially during Qingming. Sometimes performances are put on for the spirits. Chinese opera is quite different from Western opera. It includes songs, speaking, mime, dance, and acrobatics. Actors wear colorful costumes and masks.

THINK ABOUT THIS

Halloween is a lot like the Hungry Ghosts Festival. On both days, the dead are thought to return to the world of the living. Do you know why people wear costumes on Halloween? Do you think it has something to do with keeping ghosts away?

Dragon Boats and Moon Cakes

An old man stands in a boat floating on a deep river. Holding a heavy rock, he steps overboard, quickly sinking to the river's bottom. This is the story of Qu Yuan, who drowned himself because he could not stand to see his country ruined by corrupt leaders. As the story goes, the people of a nearby village went out in their boats to search for him, but they were too late. In great sorrow, they threw rice into the water to feed the man's hungry spirit. Then one day, his spirit returned and told them that the river dragon was eating all the food meant for him. He told the villagers to wrap the rice in leaves to disguise it. Today people eat these rice dumplings at the Dragon Boat Festival to remember Qu Yuan.

✱ Dragon boating is now a popular sport around the world.

The Dragon Boat Festival

The Dragon Boat Festival takes place on the fifth day of the fifth lunar month, around midsummer. It probably started as a festival to celebrate the planting of the rice crop and to ask the gods for a good rainfall. At that time, people believed that dragon gods controlled rivers and rain. They put offerings in the river so that the dragons would bring rain for their crops.

Today the highlight of the festival is the dragon boat racing. Dragon boats are long, narrow boats with a carved dragon's head at one end and a tail at the other. Up to eighty rowers paddle together. A leader shouts directions and sets the rhythm for the rowers using a large drum. The races are very noisy and exciting to watch. Teams try to trick each other into a wrong move in order to win the race.

✳ Dragon boat races are very competitive. If the boat's crew is not careful, the boat can easily overturn.

✳ It was believed that the dragon gods controlled the rivers, rainfall, and flooding.

The Mid-Autumn Festival

The other festival that comes from the rice-growing cycle is the Mid-Autumn Festival. The Mid-Autumn Festival was once a day of thanksgiving for the rice harvest. It was an outdoor festival in which people went out to the valleys and mountains to hike and picnic. Today the Mid-Autumn Festival is still spent outdoors, but now it is a celebration of the moon and the beauty of autumn.

According to the Chinese calendar, autumn falls on the seventh, eighth, and ninth months of the year. The Mid-Autumn Festival takes place on the fifteenth day of the eighth month, in the middle of autumn on the night of the full moon. On this night, the moon is at its roundest and brightest. It is a time to sit outside with friends and family, enjoy the moonlight, and eat moon cakes.

A farmer tends to his rice paddy in rural China. The Mid-Autumn Festival takes place after the harvest, when farmers have free time to enjoy the cool autumn weather and the beauty of nature.

Try A Moon Cake

The most common moon cakes are those with a brown skin and a sweet brown paste filling, but there are many different kinds. Some are sweet and others are not. Moon cakes used to come in all sorts of shapes—**pagodas**, horses, fish, and other animals. Today they are usually round, with Chinese symbols in the middle.

Most moon cakes are brown, but some are white or even green. The most popular moon cakes have fillings made of egg yolk, lotus seed paste, or coconut.

Moon Cakes Save the Day

Some people think moon cakes are partly responsible for a rebellion against the **Mongols** at a time when China was under Mongol rule. Legend has it that the rebel army commander sent moon cakes to the people of one town a few days before the Mid-Autumn Festival. On the night of the festival, the people found notes in the moon cakes telling them to rise up and fight the Mongols at midnight. When the time came, the people attacked. The rebel army joined them and the city was freed from Mongol rule.

The Lady in the Moon

People retell many legends about the moon at the Mid-Autumn Festival. One of the popular stories is about the lady in the moon. One version of the story tells about ten suns that suddenly appeared in the sky. The heat of the suns was so intense that it angered the emperor. The emperor ordered one of his best archers, Hou Yi, to shoot down the extra suns. Hou Yi shot down all but one. He was rewarded with a special potion that would allow him to live forever, but he had to wait twelve months before he could take it. One day while he was out, his wife, Chang Er, found the potion. She swallowed it and was suddenly able to fly. To escape her husband's anger, she flew to the moon. According to the myth, she still lives there today.

The figure of Chang Er, the lady in the moon.

Tibetan New Year

Tibetans have a culture that is very different from Chinese culture. More than fifty years ago, Tibet became part of China, but the Tibetans have kept many of their own traditions alive. One of these is *Losar*, the Tibetan New Year. In some ways, Losar is similar to the Chinese New Year. Before the New Year, the house must be thoroughly cleaned and special meals prepared for the New Year's Day feast. Visiting friends is a big part of the celebration. However, there are other traditions that are only followed in Tibet.

Let's Dance

Tibetans follow a special kind of Buddhism called **Lamaism**. Their religion is very important to them. Most of their celebrations take place in the temple. For part of the New Year's celebrations, monks dress in masks and costumes. They put on dances at the temple to show the struggle between good and evil. It takes a lot of practice to do these dances. According to legend, one monk was able to make rocks explode and set robes on fire through his dancing.

✳ A monk performs a dance for the New Year's celebrations.

Sweeping Away the Demons

Tibetans have a special practice to get rid of any demons that might have settled in their house. On the last night of the year, the house is swept and any dirt is left in a pile in the corner. On top of the pile, they put little models of demons made out of dough. Then the women braid their hair and everyone dresses in new clothes. The family then sits down to eat a special meal.

After they have finished eating, everyone in the family helps to pick up the pile of dirt and the demons. They carry the dirt and demons outside to a big fire. All the neighbors bring their piles of dirt, too. They throw the dirt and demons on the fire, and everyone shouts and sets off fireworks to scare the demons back to their world.

✳ *Thangkas* are paintings made on fabric. The hanging of the thangka before a festival is an important ceremony. Some are so big that it takes dozens of monks to carry them and hang them in position.

✳ The second day of the new year is full of religious ceremonies. Here, a temple visitor makes an offering to a monk.

Things for You to Do

The Chinese believe that each year is ruled by one of twelve animals. People have the characteristics of the animal that ruled the year they were born. Find out what kind of animal you are by looking for the year you were born. Then read the description of your animal's traits. Does the description fit? The Chinese characters next to each animal give the name of the animal in Chinese.

RATS are bright, sociable, happy, and charming but can also be excitable.

1960, 1972, 1984, 1996, 2008

OXEN are hardworking and dependable, steady, and trustworthy. They like to follow rules.

1961, 1973, 1985, 1997, 2009

DRAGONS are full of strength and energy, and always on the go. They love a colorful life and set high standards in everything they do.

1952, 1964, 1976, 1988, 2000, 2012

TIGERS are powerful, passionate, and daring. They are also rebellious and unpredictable.

1950, 1962, 1974, 1986, 1998, 2010

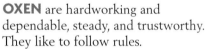

SNAKES are wise, clever, and soft-spoken. They like good books and deep thoughts. They dress well and can be vain.

1953, 1965, 1977, 1989, 2001

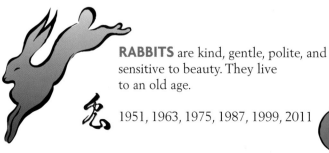

RABBITS are kind, gentle, polite, and sensitive to beauty. They live to an old age.

1951, 1963, 1975, 1987, 1999, 2011

HORSES are very attractive, with a lot of appeal. They are talkative and sensitive. They are adaptable and may fall in love easily.

1954, 1966, 1978, 1990, 2002

MONKEYS are quick-witted and charming but may be deceitful. They are inventive and can be successful at almost anything, especially languages.

1956, 1968, 1980, 1992, 2004

SHEEP are tender, sympathetic, and are often shy. They can easily become overwhelmed by life.

1955, 1967, 1979, 1991, 2003

ROOSTERS are a little too sure of themselves. They are proud and handsome. Some roosters talk all the time and are funny; others are more serious and direct.

1957, 1969, 1981, 1993, 2005

DOGS are very likeable. They are honest, sincere, loyal, and intelligent. They like things to be fair and just.

1958, 1970, 1982, 1994, 2006

PIGS are honest and brave. They can accept the hard things in life and never hold a grudge.

1959, 1971, 1983, 1995, 2007

FURTHER INFORMATION

Books: *Chinese Festivals—Celebrating the Mid-Autumn Festival.* Sanmu Tang (Better Link Press, 2008).

Chinese New Year. Ann Heinrichs (Child's World, 2006).

If I Were a Kid in Ancient China. Cobblestone Publishing (Cricket Books, 2007).

Websites: www.china.org.cn/english/features/Festivals/78131.htm—Further information about China's history and traditional Chinese festivals.

www.chinatour.com/countryinfo/festival.htm—Includes detailed information about China and its many exciting festivals.

www.new-year.co.uk/chinese/—Provides information about Chinese New Year.

Make a Dragon Kite

You can make your own dragon kite for Qingming Day. Draw your own dragon or use the one on the page for inspiration. Red and yellow are **auspicious** colors for a dragon—and they make a beautiful kite!

You will need:

1. Crêpe paper rolls in three colors
2. Thread or string
3. Poster paint
4. Paintbrushes
5. A pencil
6. Scissors
7. Tissue paper
8. Glue
9. Craft knife and an adult's help
10. Three foot-long dowels, or sticks

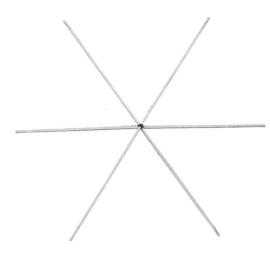

1 Arrange the dowels like this. Use the thread to tie them together in the middle.

2 Ask an adult to carefully cut small slits in the ends of the dowels.

3 Tie the thread around the edges of the kite, using the slits to hold it in place.

4 Cut the tissue paper to fit around the kite shape with a small flap on each edge. Paint a dragon face on the paper. Lay the frame over the paper. Put glue on the flaps and then fold them down.

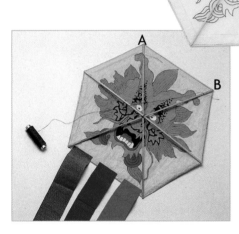

5 Cut two pieces of thread about 8 inches (20 centimeters) long. Tie them to points A and B. Tie the end of the rest of the thread to the center. Then tie the two short pieces to the long thread to make a harness. Glue crêpe paper streamers to the bottom of the kite. You're ready to fly!

Make Tang Yuan

Tang yuan is a sweet dessert that is eaten at the Winter Solstice Festival. It's also offered to ancestors as a symbol of family reunion. Tang yuan is a popular treat, especially with children, and it's easy to make. This recipe makes enough for four people.

You will need:
1. 2 cups (280 g) rice flour
2. 3 cups (400 g) brown sugar
3. 6 cups (1.44 l) water
4. Red, green, and yellow food coloring
5. Ladle
6. Wooden spoon
7. Measuring cup
8. Saucepan
9. Large bowl

1 Mix 1 cup (240 ml) water and the flour together in a bowl.

3 Mix the sugar into 5 cups (1.2 l) of water in a saucepan. Ask your adult helper to heat the sugar water over medium-high heat.

5 Roll the dough into balls the size of large marbles. Then drop them into the sugar water. Ask an adult to help you cook them until they rise to the top. Serve the balls in the syrup. You can eat them hot or cold.

2 With clean hands, pick up the dough and knead it for a few minutes.

4 Divide the dough into three lumps. Add a different color to each, working it in until the dough is colored all the way through. Make sure you wash your hands before switching lumps!

Glossary

ancestor	A family member who came before.
auspicious	Bringing good luck.
Buddhism	A religion based on the teachings of Buddha in which people are taught self-control.
Han Chinese	The main group of people in China.
hongbao	A red envelope with money inside given at New Year.
incense	A substance that when burned gives off a sweet smell.
kumquat	A small orange fruit with a sour taste.
Lamaism	The Tibetan form of Buddhism.
lunar	Following the phases of the moon.
martial arts	Traditional Asian forms of self-defense.
Mongols	People from Central Asia who live in Mongolia.
Muslim	A follower of Islam.
pagoda	A tower with roofs that curve upward.
Taoism	A religion that teaches people to follow the way of the world.

Index

Photo Credits
Alamy/Photolibrary: 6 (top), 14 (top),
19, 21 (bottom), 22, 25 (bottom); Bes
Stock: 5; Getty Images: 6 (bottom),
7 (top), 8 (bottom), 20 (bottom), 23
(bottom), 24; HBL Network Photo
Agency: 3 (bottom); Hong Kong Tourist
Board: 9 (bottom), 12 (bottom), 16,
21 (top); Hutchison Library: 15, 17
(top), 18; Image Bank: cover, 1, 2, 4,
7 (bottom), 10 (both), 12 (top), 13
(both), 14 (bottom); Photolibrary:
11, 25 (top); Shandong International
Tourism Board: 28 (top); Singapore
Tourist Promotion Board: 17 (bottom)